snake & stone

Natalie Morison-Uzzle

Hampton Roads, Va., Wider Perspectives Publishing

The writings herein are the product of Natalie Morison-Uzzle, and she is responsible for the contents. Wider Perspectives Publishing reserves 1st run rights of this work and all rights revert to the author upon delivery. Author then reserves the right to grant or restrict reprinting of this volume in whole or in part and may resubmit for contests and anthologies at will.

1st run released March 2020

Copyright Natalie Morison-Uzzle, 2020
March 2020, Richmond, Va. By way of Norfolk, Va./Wider Perspectives Publishing
1st ed. ISBN 9798630279972
2nd ed. (2020) ISBN: **978-1-952773-06-8**

Acknowledgement

To my dear friends, my always encouraging grandparents, and everyone who told me I had something special- thank you. I am so grateful the universe placed each of you on my path.

Contents

No Men on the Moon	2
Masochist in the Mirror	4
Mommy Issues	6
I Call it Magic	8
Sister of the Sea	10
A Cigarette for Venus	12
Stage Slut	14
Apartment 33	16
Mother Mary on Guitar	18
Birthday	20
Hollow	22
Snake & Stone	24
Holy Soul	26

NO MEN ON THE MOON

It may have been the summer of '69 but he gave nothing in return.
He conquered her surface without consent
    as millions roared in pleasure.
He thrust himself upon her and stomped across her craters.
He stabbed his country's star spangled ego, steel rodded pride
    into her powdered, gray flesh.
And then flew 525 stars away.

But he was not the first.
No.
We were there. Always.
My mother, my great-great-grandmother.
That woman I wanted to touch with my tongue but never did.
She's there along with every native woman raped by men
    who'd never once kissed the land they pilfered.
Even when the wind did nothing but stroke their hair and whisper
meekly in their ears.

They are there.
So is she.
And her.
You are too, woman.
You are too.

The moon is where we come from and the moon is where we stay.
She bleeds our blood and births our children
    and never looks the other way.
She feels what we feel as we feel it and knows when to call our names.
She pulled you crying from your mother's womb
And fed you your intuition, milky white and true.

She put the pink in your nipples and the hard on your heels.
So you could walk the sands of time as you fed the earth's children.
She put extra water behind your obsidian eyes
To cry for every man who can't find a tear.
She carved your fangs herself as the wolves howled below in ecstasy,
excited to call you a sister.

Yet I won't bite back.
I don't feast on the pleasure prompted.
I am still flossing last night's ignorance from my teeth,
tasting the tingle of impetuous mint,
rinsing with synthetically flavored sympathy.

No, women- we will not sink our teeth in.
When they turn their backs on us again we will land on the sun,
Every man's favorite star.
And we will laugh and scream and laugh
Because you can't fuck a woman on fire,
You can only watch her burn.

MASOCHIST IN THE MIRROR

Tonight I could make a zero look full
Break me
Open.
Like tree branches waiting
for their wind
their rain
their thunder.
With a cum-hither motion
won't you finger out this parasite
that carves away at me
unsparingly?

Trembling needles push ink
under millennial skin, cutting
a dark and silent fable in.
And as the pain surfaces
for a moment I forget to breathe
until I remember
I'm getting exactly what I wanted

Just like I want all these hungry men to want me
as I weave them into the silken sheets
of a black widow bed
swaddling them like babies without heads
writing words with spider hands
in a spiral language only Charlotte can understand
because the architect knows exactly how to destroy her own temple.
She has carnal knowledge of every crack
in her red earth foundation.

Is there not a dark catharsis in blowing your own house down?
Do you not feel sweet relief when a brick forgets its shape?
When a rectangle forgets its walls?
Don't you like to watch clay
crumble?

I wake sore in the morning, flesh burning
like a monk who set himself on fire
in protest
of his own busted heart.

I can't utter a word
I can't even cry
and for a moment
I forget to breathe
until I catch a glimpse
of the masochist
in the mirror
and I remember
we're getting exactly what we wanted.

MOMMY ISSUES

Jacob's was a psychopath,
Dillon's was in prison
Andrew's chose her husband
and Kevin's turned out to like women.
Michael was a nympho who performed for love,
but a girl he could not keep.
His body was his pride and joy, the peak was his relief.

They would lay their broken heads upon my bosom
    as hungry babies feed.
I needed them to need me, just as mothers need.
They got their bottles from the liquor store
    and drank them dry too much.
A mother's milk would never be enough, nor a mother's touch.
Clonazepam was their goodnight kiss and weed their Sunday brunch.

All were growing numb, sucking on their acid thumbs,
    lost in its disease.
Tripping, tripping until they stumbled
    and the feelings seemed to cease.
Drugs can't make it better but boys,
you may not cry.
Suck it in the form of smoke and let it out as "guy"
Fuck a little harder, take X instead of E.
If you toughen yourself from the inside
it might burn a little less.

I loved you each and when my mom died
I had mommy issues too.
The difference though is simple
I'll always need my mom,
I never needed you.

I CALL IT MAGIC

What is making that chime... chime?
I don't see anything.
It's picking up leaves and spinning them
howling at my window in the night
like the original wolf
It moves plastic lawn chairs into strange corners while we sleep
and yet we think nothing of it?

When it's angry
it will not hesitate to toss whole houses into the sky,
raining them down in parts
It molds cloud scraping waves,
thrashing furious water onto apologetic land

It's a spirit in my ears,
my grandmother gently brushing back my hair,
kissing my cheeks in the cold,
blowing on my hot face as the cicadas sing in July.

An invisible force,
moving old trees,
crying out like a forgotten poltergeist.
Some call it wind.

I call it magic.

SISTER OF THE SEA

I'm talking in my sleep
to tell you things before we meet
and I can't stop dreaming
of holding your hand
when I wake from visions
of us on land
of stable houses,
a stable man

When her turquoise soul
left her body,
your body needed hers.
Your body hadn't learned what it meant
to bleed a garnet river
for seven days straight
somehow
without dying

You would splish splash
in your childhood tears
while I swam through waves
of adolescent anger

An ocean of grief
overfloweth between us
until I swam ashore with salted wounds
and wet leaf feet
and howled through years of trees;
"Mother, mother is in the mountains!"

You kept on swimming
treading saltwater
gasping for air
grasping at our gone mother's hair

Sister
sister of the sea
I fear that you may drown
before your legs come to meet me

A CIGARETTE FOR VENUS

A year after I extinguished the final flame
sacrificing one last Newport in your driveway,
crushing its tobacco spine between my thumb and index finger
you call to apologize for being elusive.

Like the smoke you thrust from bearded lips
even as it caressed the tiny ridges of your throat
kissing your lungs so deeply
unfurling into every rounded corner.

Speechless.
I am
as this flame-thrower has the audacity to say
I set the bar.
Pulling out his lighter to light me up
and hand me off.
To her
so she can learn to suck
smoke like me.

I want to know why
no one ever asks the "one that got away" what it feels like to escape
the fire she half-started.
To stand alone, empty handed and on display
like an unarmed statue
carved out by some man too wrapped around himself
to hug another.

If you asked Venus de Milo
she would crack open her ancient stone lips
wag her wise marble tongue and say
she is tired of being the woman for all your new women to look up to,
exhausted of being the one left loveless
after you find another to put your love into -

Her.
The woman old enough to be your age
the mother of two who has no idea
you're texting me, saying
a piece of your heart will forever
have my name

You remember
Fire in the bed,
on the dining room table
kitchen counter
living room couch
back porch
bare wall
hardwood floor
picnic blanket
earth.

Will you ask Rachel to mail me a cigarette
before I burn down that already smoldering
gas powered
neatly contained
fireplace fire?

I won't tell her you called.

STAGE SLUT

Legs cracked open like morning eggs; curtains spread
I'm pouring out
onto you, into you.
My mouth agape, your eyes wide.

I'm taking off everything I own for you,
    stripped down to the soul for you
because your applause make me whole,
sewing up the empty holes birds call home.
Nesting in your eyes- security.
A stranger's affinity.

Come and get it
I'm hot off the press, bleeding at the breast.
I started young and I can't stop.
Lick the salt off my skin before another poem begins
because you're swimming in an unpublished ocean,
witnessing a virgin poet in motion.
Don't wave.
Just clap your hands and say my name.

I don't want dollar bills, I want to be on your bookshelf
bound and in good health.
Lips wet, tongue wagging,
I'm a stage slut in my pen to paper prime.
Mic me while I preach my truth.

APARTMENT 33

The only thing I love more than the sound of my neighbor fucking his girlfriend is the sound of them fighting.
The only thing I love more than the sound of them fighting is hearing his music late at night.
The only thing I love more than hearing his music is listening to him sing on guitar, "My love is so big."
The only thing I love more than him apologizing over song, is hearing his girlfriend shriek, "You don't love me." repeatedly.
The only thing I love more than hearing a woman scream she is not loved, is hearing the two make up using only their bodies on Sunday morning
The only thing I love more than carnal reconciliation is watching a movie with no pictures in clouds above my head,
wondering how did I get so lucky in love
To be alone.

MOTHER MARY ON GUITAR

I couldn't connect to him
with his erect and unforgiving steeples
busting through the trees
before I was ready to see
I didn't need a holy father,
I needed a mother.

Chan, soul bared, nude as the news
Lana, with her snug blue jeans and melancholy eyes
Florence, with those smoldering red locks and lungs full of something
and Courtney, with strong hands and smudged lips;
my mothers of song

Rock goddesses can bleed without dying
windows down, voices flying
like angels high on cocaine wings
I would turn up the volume, bow my head and pray
to a violet queen in an amethyst sky
as gospel leaked from the mouths of women
who were loud enough to hear
my cries in some fallen down, suburban town.
At 13 I was instructed to suck the dick
of an invisible man miles above me,
they promised that Jesus loved me.
"Save yourself for him. He wants you to."
"*He wants you too.*"

Well I want his wife a little more and
wasn't he in love with dying?
Does it matter when all these skater boys are still praying
to a 90's god with a bullet in his head,
pointing fingers at his wife for something she said?

I'll spread my legs for Cat Power,
the witches who don't cower
the women clutching my throat through the stereo
screaming
"SPEAK!"
"Claw their fucking eyes out to help them see!"
God is a woman preaching on the radio
who will teach you everything you need to know
about men that convinced you oral devotion was owed

They will push your head down
Lower
Lower...
You will brush off your knees
walk to the woods
and open your CD case
Leaning on lyric book salvation
saying
AMEN
Aman
A man
did this to me.

Mother Mary will pick up her guitar
Eve will find the courage to amplify her forbidden fruit voice
and they will play
until the sky cries golden rain

When   will   women   stop   kneeling   for   men   below   them?

BIRTHDAY

Fuck me like I'm worthless
Fuck me like I'm priceless
Fuck me while you write a poem in your head
about two pristine lips attached to
one dirty mouth
in which the reddest of roses grew

How the noises I make have you coming thrice
before the echo can hit the paint

Fuck me like the skin I scrape from your back
    is all the sugar we have left for coffee
and that sugar is made of diamonds
Fuck me so quietly my pinky toe screams for all the mice to hear
Fuck me like the day the doctor pulled you out
and you knew you wanted back in

HOLLOW

I'm scared of lonely poems
because I'm scared
I'll feel more lonely if I write one.
Honestly, I'm tired
of taking myself out
to lunch at empty restaurants
with fancy glasses
watching couples feed each other pastry
in spaces I hold sacred.

Going to the grocery store
looking at men
with wedding ringed fingers
as they bite their wives' ears near
Sunkist lemons.
I'm getting older.

My friend is having a baby
and I'm not sure what to think
after a psychic said I died in childbirth
and lived
in the skin of a Scottish midwife
who never once lost a baby.

I am pregnant with this book
the one kicking at my side
so persistently,
since I was sixteen.
I just want to show the world that I can make something
without pushing my body into someone else's.

But yes, it would be nice
to have two sets of keys for one door
two heads at my headboard
or to see a table set for two
and he's cooking.

I have been ravenous my whole life.
I was always hungry
when my family was full.
My parents said
I was born with a hollow leg
What then, would they call my heart?

SNAKE & STONE

She built an empire of snake and stone,
circle and sun,
mountains and rust,
of magnolia tree seeds
and seagull feathers
She built an empire off the backs of broken bricks,
Forging a nest in rented walls.

Earth became clay and she asked with her third eye
can I build a home
in the sky?
With flesh colored tears pink hands bled red
as she turned liquid life solid,
foxes into family
Eggs held unborn hopes
like yolked dreams
hatching with eyes closed
behind flickering eyelids

In the words of a woman who must shed her skin
again
again
again
to see that serpents were always friends
hissing her name
writing it in the summer air
with their sparkler tongues,
tying knots with their cold, rope bodies
tethering me to me.
Until I came home to myself
looked up at the sky
and saw that I was rich.

I built an empire.

HOLY SOUL

The rain today blends with the rain of yesterday,
the day before that
and I think of all the things I can't let go of.
My favorite boots with a hole in the soul.
My left gets wet and my right wonders why.

There's just so much music in those shoes
so many hands held
hearts trampled
fits of rage
tantrums of laughter
spilt drinks
lovers fucked
earth massaged.

Worn thin by my weight on the world or its weight on me
And I think of every right turn I made until I crashed, full speed,
    into myself.
What does that feel like?
A lot of things.
Sometimes it's pedaling home in the pouring rain,
looking in the mirror
hair dripping, thinking
G   O   D
She's so fucking beautiful.

I keep remembering at the pub
how a stranger saw straight through a girl
in a see-through top.
He saw my mesh-covered misery and
we kissed
because sad souls
like to sink their teeth in

I wish I could tell him I'm better
That I found water, I'm growing
and soon I might bloom.

I've been thinking about
everything I can't let go of
like my favorite boots.
My left gets wet and my right understands
I'm the happiest I've ever been
with a hole in my soul.

Your Author

Natalie is an art therapist by day and a poet by night. She began reading her work at open mics while attending graduate school in Norfolk, Virginia. She now resides in Richmond, Virginia where she continues to put down her literary roots. *Snake & Stone* is her first poetry publication.

colophon
Brought to you by Wider Perspectives Publishing, care of James Wilson, with the mission of advancing the poetry and creative community of Hampton Roads, Virginia.
See our production of works from …

Tanya Cunningham-Jones
    (Scientific Eve)
Terra Leigh
Ray Simmons Samantha Borders-Shoemaker
Taz Waysweete'
Bobby K.
    (The Poor Man's Poet)
J. Scott Wilson (TEECH!)
Charles Wilson
Gloria Darlene Mann
Neil Spirtas
Zach Crowe
Jorge Mendez & JT Williams
Sarah Eileen Williams
    Stephanie Diana (Noftz)
the Hampton Roads
    Artistic Collective
Jason Brown (Drk Mtr)
Martina Champion
Tony Broadway
Ken Sutton
Crickyt J. Expression
Lisa M. Kendrick
Cassandra IsFree
Nich (Nicholis Williams)
Gloria Darlene Mann

   … and others to come soon.

We promote and support the artists of the 757
from the seats, from the stands,
from the snapping fingers and
    clapping hands
from the pages, and the stages
and now we pass them forth
    to the ages

Check for the above artists on FaceBook, the Virginia Poetry Online channel on YouTube, and other social media.

Hampton Roads Artistic Collective is the non-profit extension of WPP and strives to simultaneously support worthy causes in Hampton Roads and the creative artists.

www.ingramcontent.com/pod-product-compliance
Lightning Source LLC
Chambersburg PA
CBHW031219090426
42736CB00009B/989